COLLEGE Qs:

ROOMMATES

50 QUESTIONS TO ASK YOUR ROOMMATE
(SO YOU DON'T HATE EACH OTHER AT THE END OF THE YEAR)

K. NICOLE

College Qs: Roommates

Copyright © 2021 by Kaliyah Martin.

Typeset and printed in the United States of America.

ISBN: 978-0-578-95153-9 (Paperback)

For all the soon-to-be college roommates, here's to hoping you don't hate each other at the end of the year.

TABLE OF CONTENTS

INTRODUCTION

POV: You're a college student with a roommate you have to live with for the rest of the year and you don't want to hate them.

I'll keep this blurb brief because let's face it, you just care about the questions (see the section titled Complete List of All the Qs if you really don't wanna wait).

If you're reading this because you're hoping these questions will magically guarantee that you and your roommates will be besties and never argue and be the roommates-turned-friends that everyone wishes they were... I'm sorry to burst your bubble. Actually, no, I'm not sorry. This is the (young) adult world. You might as well get used to reality.

The truth is you might not be best friends with your roommate, even if your roommate is your best friend going into this whole rooming situation. Best friends don't always make the best roommates, and the best roommates don't always become best friends. That's okay. The best roommates are simply people who live really well together. Best friends or not. By the end of this book, you'll have just about everything you'll need to at the bare minimum set yourself up for peacefully coexisting with the person (or people) you'll be living with for the next year.

GETTING TO KNOW YOU QS

GETTING TO KNOW YOU QUESTIONS

Step 1 in ensuring you and your roommate/s don't hate each other is breaking the ice and getting to know each other a bit. If you've known your roommate/s forever, you might want to skip over this part. Or don't. It could be a fun friendship test. Either way, no one wants to be that awkward person who forgot their roommate's birthday or said "Merry Christmas" when, in fact, your roommate is Jewish.

No need to get deep (unless you're into that sort of thing and the conversation naturally flows there). Remember, the primary goal is not to force a best friendship. Just be chill, and get to know each other on a basic level.

THE QS:

1. Are you more of an introvert or extrovert?
2. What is your major and why'd you choose this college?

3. What do you like to do in your free time (i.e. passions/hobbies/pastimes)?

4. Do you have any shows you'd want to binge watch or favorite movies?

> *Qs 3 and 4 are a good starting place for you to see if you and your roommate can find some things to do together. Don't freak out if you seemingly don't have anything in common. They can still be an amazing roommate even if you like True Crime and all they watch is To All The Boys on repeat.*

5. Do you have any important beliefs or morals?

> *I know this q might seem a little deep, but it doesn't have to be. Some people have strong personal convictions. It might also be nice to see which of these personal convictions are things your roommate might feel uncomfortable with if you did them in the room. It is better to learn this sooner rather than after you've unintentionally crossed their boundary and get smacked with a wave of pettiness and passive aggression.*

6. What holidays do you like to celebrate and when's your birthday?

> *If you're bad with dates, maybe put their birthday on your phone calendar or something, especially if it's during the semester. This is also the q where you might find out that your roommate is Jewish and that you probably shouldn't be wishing them a Merry Christmas (Happy Holidays is definitely the pc preference anyway if you're into that kind of thing).*

BED + SLEEPING HABITS QS

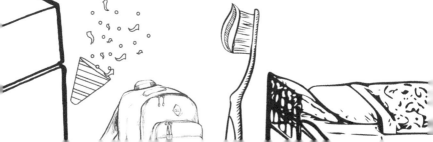

BED AND SLEEPING HABITS QUESTIONS

Sleep is a coveted thing in college, so you'll definitely want to make sure you're respecting each other's hours of slumber. I'd advise asking these sets of qs sooner rather than later in case any of these are deal-breakers.

THE QS:

1. Are you a morning person or a night owl?
2. What time do you like to wake up/go to bed on weekdays versus weekends?
3. Are you a heavy sleeper or a light sleeper?
4. Be honest, do you do any weird things in your sleep (i.e. snore, sleep walk, sleep talk)?

QUICK STORY TIME

My freshman year of college, I had two roommates. One of them talked in their sleep. The other one was a sleepwalker. As you can imagine, nighttime was very eventful. Thankfully, I wasn't a light sleeper so it didn't bother me, but that could have been a deal-breaker for someone else.

5. If I see that you've slept past your alarm and might be late to class, do you want me to wake you up?

6. Is your bed off limits to me and/or any guests?

College rooms can be small, and your room might not have space for a futon or air mattress or extra sleeping accommodations should you have a guest in your room. If your roommate is out of town for the weekend and you have a guest that same weekend, your roommate might be cool with you sleeping in their bed so you can let your guest sleep in yours. Maybe your roommate is super cool with your guest sleeping in their bed. This is assuming your roommate is cool with you having guests sleep in the room (see Social Life Qs). Either way, it's a good thing to ask first

7. Do you want to keep our beds on the ground, bunk, or loft them?

CLEANLINESS QS

CLEANLINESS QUESTIONS

*Cleanliness qs are another super important set of qs to ask sooner rather than later. Cleaning schedules, or the lack thereof, and messiness is often the source of most roommate passive aggression and pettiness. After going through these qs, it might be helpful for you and your roommate/s to create some sort of Cleaning Schedule. Some living arrangements require and provide one; others don't. Whatever your situation, there's some guidance in the **College Roommate Agreement** to get you started.*

THE QS:

1. What does your room at home usually look like?
2. Are you normally a messy person or a neat freak? Rate yourself on a scale from 1-10.
3. How often do you like to clean?
4. How often do you like to clean the bathroom or shared equivalent (i.e. sink)?
5. Are you cool w/ a messy sink (i.e. toothpaste, hair shedding, etc.)?

Sinks get dirty very quickly from shedding, toothpaste globs, makeup residue, etc. Maybe at your home you're used to having your own sink, and maybe in college, you'll have your own too so it won't be too much of an issue. If it is a shared sink, you may want to evaluate how cool you are with seeing another person's sink gunk.

6. Do you shave in the sink or the shower? Both?
7. Do you get sick easily?

QUICK STORY TIME

College is like daycare, germs spread quickly. My freshman year of college, almost everyone caught what people on campus called 'The Plague'. I don't get sick, so I didn't catch it even when both of my roommates had it. Although in a post-pandemic world people are a little more conscious of how germs travel, this is still a good conversation to have with your roommate/s because the tolerance of their immune system might be different than yours. PRO TIP that you didn't ask for, but I'm going to give you anyway about staying healthy in college --- EmergenC or other vitamin C supplements are your best friends. It's much easier to fight that tickle in your throat with daily doses of EmergenC and maybe even a few cough drops before it becomes a stuffy nose and violent hacking cough. A mini air purifier, if it's in your budget, also doesn't hurt.

BOUNDARIES Q5

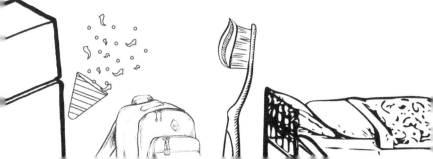

BOUNDARY QUESTIONS

If you're used to having a lot of alone time, college might be an adjustment. If you and your roommate/s share a room, and not just a common space, more times than not you won't be alone. This set of qs are important to ask so you can figure out when you can create or find some alone time for yourself and when you need to give your roommate/s space for the same.

THE QS:

1. When do you prefer to have alone time?
2. When you're upset, do you like to talk about it?

> We all need different things when we're having a rough time. Some people like to talk about it, other people need their space. If you or your roommate/s are the type that needs space and might even want the room to yourself, don't be afraid to kindly mention this in advance.

3. How much alone time do you need?

> *Obviously, don't go overboard because the room is equal parts yours and your roommate/s. You cannot kick them out for most of the day. If you are someone who needs a lot of alone time, maybe try exploring campus to find spaces outside of your room to be alone. Maybe you and your roommate/s can even have a compromise, like when you have your headphones in while you're both in the room that's a signal that you need quiet time.*

4. What kind of things annoy you or are your big pet peeves?

5. What are some boundaries you have for your side of the room?

6. What things are you cool with sharing?

7. What things are absolutely off-limits?

QUICK PERSONAL STORY TIME

I always had hella snacks in college. My parents shopped at Costco for me because they assumed that most of the snacks I had would be shared with my roommates and last most of the semester. We had a pretty open snack policy in our room, which was fine until my roommates' squad of friends started helping themselves to my snack stash too. The snacks dwindled very quickly. I was cool with my roommates eating them, and if their friends wanted a snack every once in a while that would have been okay, but I should've specified that it wasn't a communal snack stash for anyone who entered our space. Try to be as specific as possible with qs 6 and 2. Be specific about what things you are cool with sharing and who you are cool with sharing them with sooner rather than later. Be direct about this, even if it's a little hard at first. I promise it'll help you avoid very awkward, petty, or passive-aggressive confrontations later.

SOCIAL LIFE Q5

SOCIAL LIFE QUESTIONS

I'm going to preface this section with the fact that none of the below qs are meant to encourage or endorse any sort of behavior or social activities in college. Nevertheless, if you're in college you're legally an adult now. Your social life is your social life. However, it's also very important to respect your roommate/s boundaries and decisions when bringing certain activities to the room.

THE QS:

1. Do you drink alcohol?

> *Assuming you are of legal age, it is super important to ask your roommate/s about whether or not they're cool with having alcoholic drinks in the room. Some colleges have particular policies about this..*

2. Do you smoke?

> It's pretty important to ask your roommate/s if they smoke. It's equally as important to have a conversation about what, when, and where they intend to do so. Having a conversation about what spaces you're cool with smoking happening is a better discussion to have sooner than later. Like with alcohol, some colleges have particular policies about this so it's in your best interest to get on the same page.

3. Do you have a significant other (or insignificant other, situationship, etc.)?

4. Are you cool with people coming over to the room?

> As previously mentioned in Bed and Sleeping Habits Qs, college rooms can be small. It's important for you and your roommate to be on the same page about your guest policy. Be specific at first, maybe you're okay with as many guests as your room can handle on weekends but only a few people on weeknights. Whatever it is, know that it's very possible that this might change as you and your roommate/s solidify your college social life.

5. Are you cool with people spending the night in our room?

> *This is another q you should be specific about. Is your answer different for weekends versus weeknights? Is it different for different genders (some schools have specific policies about this). Either way, you and your roommate/s should be on the same page.*

6. What do you like to do for fun on the weekends?

7. Do you like to go to parties?

8. Are you okay if we host a party or pregame in our room?

9. Do you prefer to have people in our room or to go to their space?

> *You and your roommate/s might change your opinion on qs 8 and 9 throughout the year, but at least try to get on the same page at the beginning.*

10. Am I allowed to have sex on the futon and/or other common spaces?

QUICK PERSONAL STORY TIME

You may be thinking 'dang, this is a personal q', but let me tell you that this is a q that you only know you need to ask after you don't ask it. One of my college friends lived in a quad their freshman year and walked in on one of their roommates having sex on the futon in the common room. It was not the roommate who was having sex's futon and my friend ended up giving it away at the end of the year because they felt too scarred to sit on it again. Maybe you or your roommate aren't planning on having sex in your room or at all, that's fine. Either way, it's worth having the awkward conversation before you end up with stains on your futon.

SCHOOL, STUDYING, + STRESS QS

SCHOOL, STUDYING, AND STRESS QUESTIONS

Finally, the section of qs that your parents are probably the most thrilled about because, after all, you are at college to get an education. College workload and stress often hits different than high school. It's important that you and your roommate/s figure out the best schedules for one another in the first few weeks before the big assignments and real work starts.

THE QS:

1. How often will you be studying in the room, if at all, and at what times?
2. If you're comfortable sharing, what's your class schedule?

> *Knowing your roommate/s' class schedule will let you know when you have classes in the same building and can walk together. Maybe you have a few together, or maybe you have some of the same breaks in your schedule and you can grab a meal together on certain days. As previously mentioned, alone time is a rarity in college. Knowing when your roommate/s has class will also tell you when the room is empty.*

3. If you're studying in the room, do you need absolute quiet? (give context in this conversation as to what activities can happen)

> *Try to be specific about your needs. If you need absolute quiet, some compromises might need to be made (i.e. headphones or ear plugs). Another thing to be specific about during this time is if it's cool to have people over during study time, but that can be talked about with the Social Life QS.*

4. How do you respond to stress?
5. What is your idea of relaxing?

For qs 4 and 5, it's important to know this upfront because college can be stressful, especially during the first few months. Maybe your roommate/s responds to stress by crying or screaming at everyone or being reckless. Maybe your roommate needs to relax by chatting on the phone or partying. Whatever the answers are, it's good to know ahead of time so you're not caught off guard and can maybe even support them

6. Are you planning on getting a job?

Similar to the class schedule q, this will give you insight into what hours the room will be unoccupied. If your roommate/s are planning on getting a job, they might also affect when they need to wake up or what time they're coming home at night during the week.

COMMUNICATION QS

COMMUNICATION QUESTIONS

Poor communication, pettiness, and passive aggression will almost certainly contribute to you and your roommate/s hating each other at the end of the year. Learning each other's communication style before any problems arise will help reduce the chance of pettiness and passive aggression.

THE QS:

1. How do you like to resolve problems if anything comes up?
2. What kind of things cheer you up/do you do for self-care?
3. How should we notify each other if we need the room to ourselves for a while?

> *Maybe this is a text, maybe this is a sock on the door. Whatever it is, pick something that works and run with it.*

4. How should we notify each other if something is bothering one of us?

QUICK STORY TIME

I'll snitch on myself this time because I was a key example of what not to do. My roommates and I freshman year never really established a cleaning schedule, and I'm a very anti-conflict person. Their friend squad was often in our common room (and yes, this is the same squad who liked to eat my snacks). Almost every week, our common room trash would be overflowing, gross, and smelly. One day, I walked into the room and it was gross, overflowing, and didn't have a trash bag. There was sticky melted ice cream crusted on the bottom and other disgusting things that made the room smell like crap. In true anti-conflict and petty form, I took a picture of the trash can and the contents of the trash that I had just emptied into a very large bag. Then I attached the photos to a very passive-aggressive note that requested that my roommates and their friends remember to empty the trash, remember to use a trash bag, and not be filthy animals. I then taped the note above the trash can. Please do not do this. Figure out before stuff like this occurs how to best address conflict and commit to it. Even if it's awkward or hard. Please don't be petty.

ROOM
AESTETHICS QS

Room Aesthetics Questions

For the rest of the year, the space that you and your roommate/s share will be home. If possible, try to coordinate on the big things like appliances and any furniture. No need to get matching stuff like bedspreads and whatnot (unless you want to), but get hype! This is probably both yours and their first time getting to decorate a living space.

THE QS:

1. Do you want to coordinate anything for the room?

You'll want to figure out what stuff each of you is going to bring so you don't end up with multiples of things. Some places come equipped with mini-fridges and microwaves, other places don't. Coordinate who is going to bring what (i.e. microwave, futon, tv, mini-fridge, etc.) before you get to campus.

2. What temperature are you most comfy in?

> This seems like a small thing, but you might be used to your living space being a certain temperature because of where you're from. That temperature might change throughout the day. For example - My roommates and I all liked to sleep in the cold so at night we opened the windows and ran the box window fans (because our dorm room didn't have A/C...I know... R.I.P). There are definitely compromises here as well if you don't agree (bed fans and space heater may get you where you need to be).

3. Would you be cool with potentially rearranging some things in our room in the future?

> The way you originally set up the living space, might not be the most ideal situation later in the year. See if your roommate/s are cool with mixing it up a bit. Maybe you thought you wanted the lofted bed at the beginning of the year, but after nearly giving yourself a concussion for the third night in a row you are regretting that decision.

Having a good roommate situation really comes down to two c words. Communication and compromise. Hopefully these q's will get the conversation started. Don't be afraid to voice your opinion if you disagree or have an alternative perspective. It's better to be firm upfront than to have regrets later when your boundaries are being crossed. To help further facilitate healthy roommate communication, check out the **Roommate Agreement** section. Some colleges require them, others don't, but it's super helpful to have an objective source of truth to return to when a conflict comes up. Last of all, remember, you don't have to be best friends to be the best roommates. Focus on living well together and anything else that comes from that is a happy bonus.

ROOMMATE
AGREEMENT

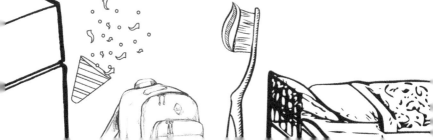

ROOMMATE AGREEMENT

THE ROOMMATES. This Roommate Agreement (the "Agreement") is between _____\(the "Roommates") all of whom agree to the following:

ROOM LOCATION. This Agreement is between the Roommates attending _____ (the "School") who are residing at the following address: _____ (the "Residence").

The responsibilities and ground rules agreed upon by the Roommates include, but are not limited to the following:

STUDY TIMES. Quiet study times (i.e. no music, guests, etc.) in the Residence are needed between the hours of _____:____ ☐ AM ☐ PM and _____:____ ☐ AM ☐ PM

☐ All Weekdays

☐ Only these specific days: ☐ M ☐ T ☐ W ☐ TH ☐ F ☐ Sat ☐ Sun

The above study times:

☐ Applies to Midterms/Finals Week

☐ Does not include Midterms/Finals Week (during these weeks, quiet hours are between the hours of _____:___ ☐ AM ☐ PM and _____:____ ☐ AM ☐ PM)

QUIET HOURS. Quiet hours for sleep without interference from noise, music, or guests are needed between the hours of _____:___ ☐ AM ☐ PM and _____:___ ☐ AM ☐ PM.)

The aforementioned sleep times:

☐ Include weekends.

☐ Does not include weekends (on weekends, from _____:___ ☐ AM PM ☐ until _____:___ ☐ AM ☐ PM.)

PERSONAL BELONGINGS. The Roommates will respect each other's personal belongings

These items cannot be borrowed:

_____
_____

These items can be borrowed with permission:

_____
_____

These items can be borrowed without permission:

_____
_____

CLEANING SCHEDULE*. Cleaning of the Residence will be (e.g. every Friday, every other Sunday, etc): _____

The cleaning responsibilities are as follows:

☐ All Roommates are required to clean everything at the scheduled time.

☐ Each Roommate will be assigned the following task(s):

_____

*create a cleaning schedule for more details or structure

GUEST POLICY.

Guests of the opposite sex and/or romantic interests are allowed in the Residence until__:__ ☐ AM ☐ PM.

☐ Including weekends.

☐ Does not include weekends (on weekends, until _____:____ ☐ AM ☐ PM.)

Guests in general are allowed in the Residence until _____:____ ☐ AM ☐ PM.

☐ Including weekends.

☐ Does not include weekends (on weekends, until _____:____ ☐ AM ☐ PM.)

Hosting guests overnight in the Residence is allowed for a maximum of ____ days

☐ Includes guest of the opposite sex and/or romantic interests

☐ Do not include guest of the opposite sex and/or romantic interests

DRUGS and ALCOHOL. All Roommates agree to follow the rules and regulations of the School in regard to drugs and alcohol.

DISAGREEMENTS. If any disagreements arise between the Roommates, it is agreed that these issues should be discussed in a candid and mutually respectful manner. All Roommates accept that it is okay to address any concerns with a Roommate if they are not fulfilling their part of this Agreement. Preferred forms of communication to bring up any disagreements include, but are not limited to:

☐ a casual but direct, in-person conversation

☐ a non-petty, non-passive aggressive text message

☐ other :

If any disagreement cannot be resolved, the Roommates agree to the following procedure:

– Work with an administrator or RA to find a solution to the disagreement

– Ask the RA/administrator to help the roommates implement the solution to the disagreement.

Additional Terms & Conditions.

_____
_____
_____
_____

Community living isn't easy, but each Roommate agrees to be a kind and responsible human who respects those around them and not be intentionally obnoxious.

We 'the Roommates' agree to the above conditions. Additionally, we agree that the above specific stipulations can be adjusted throughout the year if all roommates mutually agree to the change.

Roommate Signature _____ Date _____

COLLEGE QS: ROOMMATES

Print Name _____

Roommate Signature _____ Date _____

Print Name _____

Roommate Signature _____ Date _____

Print Name _____

Roommate Signature _____ Date _____

Print Name _____

Roommate Signature _____ Date _____

Print Name _____

Roommate Signature _____ Date _____

Print Name _____

Scan the below code to access a digital copy:

COMPLETE LIST
OF ALL THE QS

COMPLETE LIST
OF ALL THE QS

1. Are you more of an introvert or extrovert?

2. What is your major and why'd you choose this college?

3. What do you like to do in your free time (i.e. passions/hobbies/pastimes)?

4. Do you have any shows you'd want to binge watch or favorite movies?

5. Do you have any important beliefs or morals?

6. What holidays do you like to celebrate and when's your birthday?

7. Are you a morning person or a night owl?

8. What time do you like to wake up/go to bed on weekdays versus weekends?

9. Are you a heavy sleeper or a light sleeper?

10. Be honest, do you do any weird things in your sleep (i.e. snore, sleep walk, sleep talk)?

11. If I see that you've slept past your alarm and might be late to class, do you want me to wake you up?

12. Is your bed off limits to me and/or any guests?

13. Do you want to keep our beds on the ground, bunk, or loft them?

14. What does your room at home usually look like?

15. Are you normally a messy person or a neat freak? Rate yourself on a scale from 1-10.

16. How often do you like to clean?

17. How often do you like to clean the bathroom or shared equivalent (i.e. sink)?

18. Are you cool w/ a messy sink (i.e. toothpaste, hair shedding, etc.)?

19. Do you shave in the sink or the shower? Both?

20. Do you get sick easily?

21. When do you prefer to have alone time?

22. When you're upset, do you like to talk about it?

23. How much alone time do you need?

24. What kind of things annoy you or are your big pet peeves?

25. What are some boundaries you have for your side of the room?

26. What things are you cool with sharing?

27. What things are absolutely off-limits?

28. Do you drink alcohol?

29. Do you smoke?

30. Do you have a significant other (or insignificant other, situationship, etc.)?

31. Are you cool with people coming over to the room?

32. Are you cool with people spending the night in our room?

33. What do you like to do for fun on the weekends?

34. Do you like to go to parties?

35. Are you okay if we host a party or pregame in our room?

36. Do you prefer to have people in our room or to go to their space?

37. Am I allowed to have sex on the futon and/or other common spaces?

38. How often will you be studying in the room, if at all, and at what times?

39. If you're comfortable sharing, what's your class schedule?

40. If you're studying in the room, do you need absolute quiet? (give context in this conversation as to what activities can happen)

41. How do you respond to stress?

42. What is your idea of relaxing?

43. Are you planning on getting a job?

44. How do you like to resolve problems if anything comes up?

45. What kind of things cheer you up/do you do for self-care?

46. How should we notify each other if we need the room to ourselves for a while?

47. How should we notify each other if something is bothering one of us?

48. Do you want to coordinate anything for the room?

49. What temperature are you most comfy in?

50. Would you be cool with potentially rearranging some things in our room in the future?

Made in the USA
Middletown, DE
24 June 2023

33445349R00031